Justice

Arloa Sutter

wesleyan
publishing
house

Indianapolis, Indiana

Contents

Introduction: Justice for the Poor

There is a lot of confusion today about the responsibility of Christians to confront issues of social injustice. Politicians and church leaders have expressed concern that caring about issues of social justice will somehow lead to a government takeover of personal property and the establishment of a socialist or Marxist state. Well-meaning Christians who sincerely want to follow Christ are confused about what the Bible teaches about confronting systemic injustice. Never before has there been a more crucial need for clarity about the biblical mandate for Christians to be actively involved in seeking justice for the poor.

Every sector of society, including government, business, and academia, is trying to understand issues of poverty, youth violence, homelessness, and addiction. The Christian church, charged with the biblical mandate of reconciliation and Jesus' teachings about love for one another, should be front and center in these discussions. The conversation about justice is already happening, especially among young people. Movements are gaining momentum, and Christians are rallying to get involved and make a difference. Unfortunately, these movements often lack a solid theological foundation.

Too often Christians have lagged behind, choosing to remain isolated and unaware, while missing God's call for justice. Some have even adopted a theology and view of the Bible that seems to exempt them from concern for the poor or the causes of their situations.

Some of our churches have feared that if we participate in movements for justice, we will slip into a "social gospel" theology. This fear has deep roots in a reaction formed in fundamentalist churches in the 1930s and 1940s to the teaching of Walter Rauschenbusch. Rauschenbusch, a professor of church history at Rochester Seminary in New York, came face-to-face with oppressive poverty during his twelve-year pastorate in a Baptist church in the city.[1] He became disillusioned with capitalism and began to advocate for a kind of communism or Christian socialism. Some Christian leaders are fearful that like the swinging of a pendulum, addressing social concerns will lead us off course from personal faith rather than seeing the whole picture of the both/and teaching of Scripture regarding personal godliness and social justice.

In the last decade, the struggles of poverty and justice have touched our lives. From witnessing the poverty uncovered by natural disasters like Hurricane Katrina, the earthquake in Haiti, and the earthquake and tsunami in Japan to the rising violence in impoverished communities in the inner city, one can barely watch a newscast without being confronted with the problems of socioeconomic hardship. What is the responsibility of Christians in light of such overwhelming need? What can we do that will make a difference? What does the Bible teach about social justice?

This study guide will add to the justice conversation by setting forth a biblically based curriculum for Christians. It is my prayer that this study guide will serve as a basis for fresh discussions about living out authentic Christian faith in the context of social injustice.

Note

1. Walter Rauschenbusch, *Christianity and the Social Crisis* (London: Macmillan, 1907).

How to Use This Study Guide

This study guide is the second in a series of companion studies for my book, *The Invisible: What the Church Can Do to Find and Serve the Least of These*. If you have not already read *The Invisible*, you may want to purchase and read it before you embark on this study. You will find it a helpful backdrop to read what I learned from my personal journey into a deeper understanding of God's heart for the poor.

This study is designed in a workbook format for both individual study and group discussion. Each of the four group discussions are sub-divided into five studies for you to do on your own. If you commit to read the daily Scripture passages throughout the week and reflect on the questions which are provided at the end of each section, you will be prepared for the group discussion. You will need to devote about half an hour five times during the week for your personal study time. The larger group weekly discussion is designed to take about an hour.

At the beginning of each lesson, you will read a brief narrative to introduce the study. Then you will read Scripture passages and answer the questions provided. You may want to read the Scriptures several times in order to reflect upon their meaning. Write out your answers to the questions that follow in a journal or notebook. This will help you express your thoughts clearly. This will also allow you to add any comments or questions that may develop when you meet with your small group.

Each day, one of the verses will be highlighted for you to commit to memory. Write this verse on an index card and take it with you throughout the day. Reflect on it as you drive in the car or wait for a bus or train. Let the verse become part of the inventory of Scriptures that guide your life.

Hebrews 4:12 says that, "The word of God is alive and active. Sharper than any double-edged sword, it penetrates even to dividing soul and spirit, joints and marrow; it judges the thoughts and attitudes of the heart." Those of us who desire to follow Christ have chosen to base our decisions and lifestyles on the living and active sword of the Word of God.

The teachings of Scripture are not always easy. We don't usually like to have our thoughts and attitudes challenged. By embarking on this study, you have made the brave choice to journey closer to God's heart of love for all people. It will transform your life.

As you begin this study, pray that the Lord will give you an open heart to hear what he is saying to you personally through the Word. Pray for a willingness to be challenged by Scripture and for wisdom to know what God is calling you to be or to do as a result of this study.

Justice in the Old Testament

God is a God of justice. After the act of creation, God declared that everything in the world was good. There was no sin and sorrow, no brokenness and pain. Everything and everyone flowed together in justice and harmony, as God intended. God instructed Adam and Eve to tend to the earth and its animals and vegetation. It was all theirs to enjoy. There was just one command. They were not to eat of the Tree of Knowledge of Good and Evil. They weren't even supposed to know what evil was.

Sin wrecked all that. They disobeyed God's command, and sin came into the world. Working to eat became tedious. Weeds and thistles emerged from the ground. Brothers came into murderous conflict with one another, and fear and violence erupted. The God of justice was forced to lay out commands that would guard and protect his creation from itself. Those commands were also disobeyed. The world and its inhabitants became so corrupt that God judged it with a flood. Only Noah was found righteous and saved, but immediately upon emerging from the ark of his salvation, he also fell into sin.

Eventually, God the Father sent his Son, Jesus, to reclaim the world through his death on the cross. Through Christ, there is hope for the world to become what God intended. Christians are called by God, not only to personal faith in Christ for eternal salvation, but also to pick up the cross of Christ in this present world to do the work of establishing justice on earth.

This week, we will study passages of Scripture from the Old Testament that reveal God's heart of justice. We will see how the laws and commands of God put parameters in place that were intended to establish justice for the poor.

God's Heart for Justice

Justice is core to the character and work of God. Today, we will study passages of Scripture from the Old Testament that reveal how God intended to protect and care for the poor. We will also see God's anger at injustice. Those of us who know God will resonate with his heart for justice and recognize working for justice among the poor as God's work in the world.

1. Pray for God's light to reveal the meaning of the Scripture, and commit to the Lord to be willing to listen and obey.

2. Read Psalm 9:7–9 and 89:14. What is core to the throne and reign of God?

3. What role does God take for the oppressed?

4. Read Psalm 33:5 and Isaiah 30:18. What words describe the character of God?

5. Read Psalm 37:28 and Isaiah 61:8. What does God love and hate? What does God do for the just?

6. Read Psalm 99:4. If God has established equity, why is there such inequality in the world?

7. Read Psalm 146:5–9. List the types of people you find in this passage. What does God do for them?

8. Take a few minutes to pray asking God to give you a heart for justice.

Scripture Memory Verse

Psalm 9:9: "The LORD is a refuge for the oppressed, a stronghold in times of trouble."

Seek Justice

We saw yesterday that God's throne is established with justice, which is core to who God is. Today, we will reflect on encouragements and commands in Scripture for us to seek justice. When we act justly and advocate for others, we reflect God's heart. God also has some very harsh words for those who oppress the poor even though they are trying to be religious.

1. Pray for God's light as you study today's Scriptures. Ask God to help you know how to seek justice.

2. Read Isaiah 1:11–17. This is a harsh reprimand from God. What is God upset about?

3. What is God's response to their prayers?

4. What does God tell them to do instead?

5. Read Micah 6:8. What three things does God require?

6. Read Amos 4:1–2 and 5:11–12. What are some ways the poor might be oppressed today?

7. Read Amos 5:14–15, 21–24. What does God love and expect more than religious singing and services?

8. As we have read today, God has some very harsh words for religious people who are seeking God through prayers and offerings, yet neglecting justice. How can you and your family, church, or group

join in the work of God to "let justice roll on like a river, righteousness like a never-failing stream!" (Amos 5:24)?

9. Pray that God will show you opportunities today for you to act justly, love mercy, and walk humbly with God.

Scripture Memory Verse

Micah 6:8: "He has showed you, O man, what is good. And what does the LORD require of you? To act justly and to love mercy and to walk humbly with your God."

The Fat and Lean Sheep

Today, we will reflect on a passage from Ezekiel that describes two kinds of sheep: fat sheep and lean sheep. Let's see how God lovingly cared for the lean sheep that are weak and injured and how he responded to the fat sheep.

1. Pray that God's Word would speak to you clearly today. Ask God to impress upon your thoughts the message he wants you to receive.

2. Read Ezekiel 34:11–24. List the characteristics of the lean sheep and the fat sheep and the ways God responded to them.

3. God asked, "Is it not enough for you to feed on the good pasture?" (v. 18). What good pasture has God provided for you?

4. In what ways have you felt like you might be one of the lean sheep?

5. In what ways are you like one of the fat sheep?

6. How can you join God in caring for those who are scattered, weak, injured, or lost?

7. Take a few minutes to pray. Ask God to give you a heart of compassion for those who are weak, injured, and lost.

Scripture Memory Verse

Ezekiel 34:16: "I will search for the lost and bring back the strays. I will bind up the injured and strengthen the weak, but the sleek and the strong I will destroy. I will shepherd the flock with justice."

Defend the Cause of the Needy

The well-to-do can hire lobbyists and marketing professionals to advance their interests and make sure they get their piece of the pie. The poor don't have the resources or the social or emotional capital to fight for their own cause. God does not leave them without a voice. God instructs us to take up their cause, fight for them, and make sure their interests are advanced. Today, we will look at passages of Scripture that call us to speak up for the needy. We will reflect on how we can follow God's admonition to defend the cause of the poor and needy.

1. Pray that God will guide you as you study the Word today. Ask him to show you how you can defend the cause of the needy.

2. Read Psalm 10:12–18. What did the psalmist ask God to do?

3. Verse 14 says that victims commit themselves to God. Have you found this to be true? How?

4. Who are the fatherless in your community? Where do they live?

5. Have you found God to be their helper? How?

6. What does God see and hear?

7. Why does God defend the fatherless and the oppressed?

8. According to Proverbs 31:8–9, what are we to do on behalf of the poor, needy, and destitute?

9. According to Jeremiah 22:16, what does it mean to know God?

10. When you think of the poor and needy in your community, what would it look like to speak up for them and defend their cause?

11. Take a few minutes to pray. Ask God to show you who is effectively defending the cause of the needy in your community and how you can join them.

Scripture Memory Verse

Isaiah 1:17: "Learn to do right! Seek justice, encourage the oppressed. Defend the cause of the fatherless, plead the case of the widow."

The Year of Jubilee

In Luke 4:18–21, Jesus declared that he had been anointed by the Spirit of the Lord to preach good news to the poor, proclaim freedom for the prisoners and recovery of sight to the blind, and release the oppressed. Then he said he was to proclaim the year of the Lord's favor. Most Bible scholars think Jesus was referring to the Year of Jubilee described in the Old Testament book of Leviticus. The Year of Jubilee was the culmination of seven sets of seven Sabbath years and was to take place every fiftieth year. The Lord established a pattern for living that would ensure that every generation would have a fair chance to start over.

God did not prevent those who had gathered several parcels of land from prospering from those acquisitions, nor did he require them to give back all the wealth they had accumulated from their good fortune or hard work. What God did require, however, was that they return the land that was not originally theirs (and with it the opportunity for prosperity) to each new generation.

This returning of the land affirmed that all belonged to God and assured that no generation would be without opportunity because of the previous generation's poor management or unfortunate circumstances. Each new generation was given a chance to be who God made it to be.

In a day when so much wealth and power are in the hands of so few and many people have no opportunity at prosperity, it is especially important to consider God's heart on this matter. We have a responsibility to speak against any systemic injustice that robs a person of a chance at a better life. If people have stewarded the opportunities and blessings they have been given in a way that has prospered them, that is a good thing. But they must not ignore the plight of those who from generation to generation have been denied such opportunity. This matters to God.

Today, we will read about this Year of Jubilee and see what principles we can apply to our lives as we bring God's favor to those who struggle with generational poverty.

1. Pray for God's light as you study the Scripture today. Ask him to show you how you can bring his favor to men and women who are crushed by poverty.

2. Read Leviticus 25. Describe what was to happen on the seventh year after six years of production on the land?

3. What was to take place during the Year of Jubilee?

4. According to Leviticus 25:23 and Psalm 24:1, who actually owns the land?

5. How do you think this practice of Sabbath and Jubilee years would offset poverty?

6. What are some things we can do today to bring families out of poverty?

7. Take a few minutes to pray. Ask God to show you the people in your community who are trapped in generational poverty and how God would want you to bring favor to them.

Scripture Memory Verse

Psalm 24:1: "The earth is the LORD's, and everything in it, the world, and all who live in it."

Justice in the Old Testament

GROUP DISCUSSION GUIDE

This week we studied Scriptures that reveal God's heart for justice. God initiated a plan to restore justice to the world, and his law emphasized that we should protect and provide for the disadvantaged.

1. Open your group meeting in prayer, thanking God for the presence of the Holy Spirit and asking him to guide your discussion.

2. What thoughts, concerns, or fears do you have about the topic of justice for the poor?

3. Share any notes from this week's daily studies that were especially significant to you.

4. What did you learn about God's heart for justice this week?

5. What does God have to say to those who don't care for the poor?

6. Where in your community would you find people who struggle economically?

7. What individuals or groups in your community are addressing the needs of the poor?

8. How could your group serve the poor together?

9. Pray for those who are victims of poverty and injustice. Ask God to show your group how you can serve together to make a difference.

The gospel is the good news of Jesus. There is hope for a hurting world because God took action to bring transformation. God loved the world so much that he sent Jesus, the beloved Son, to earth. Jesus showed us how to live by living without sin, and then he was cruelly hung on a cross to die so that our sin could be forgiven. He died in our place. He then overcame sin and death by rising from the grave, triumphing over evil.

Jesus' death not only sets us free from our individual sin, but his death disarmed the power of systemic evil. According to Colossians 2:15, Jesus "disarmed the powers and authorities" and "made a public spectacle of them, triumphing over them by the cross." Because of Jesus' death on the cross, there is ultimate hope for the world. The gospel is good news for the poor because transformation on both a personal and social level has been made possible through Jesus. Jesus instructed his disciples to pray, "Your kingdom come, your will be done on earth as it is in heaven" (Matt. 6:10).

Receiving the good news of the gospel is not just a personal affirmation of Jesus' substitutionary death on the cross and hope of life in heaven after death. Embracing the gospel of Jesus involves embracing a new way of life. Living out the gospel includes meeting physical needs of broken people, releasing them from their bondage and oppression, and bringing them into an experience of God's favor in this present life. Becoming a Christ follower is more than intellectual assent to the work of Christ on the cross; it is a decision to follow Jesus in the way of the cross, a way of sacrifice and love. The gospel is indeed very good news for the poor because it means love will not only flow to them from God, but also through Christ followers. Those who follow Jesus will reflect his work by laying down their lives to care for those who would otherwise be cast aside.

The Mission of Christ to Transform the World

Jesus didn't come to bring individual salvation only. He came to transform the world. The work of Jesus is still being carried out on earth by those of us who are committed to follow him. The apostle Paul used a graphic illustration when he claimed that those who follow Jesus become his body, hands, and feet in a hurting world. Today, we will study verses from the Bible that reveal the overarching mission of Jesus to transform the world.

1. Pray for God's light as you study the Scripture today. Ask God to show how you can participate in the work of Jesus to bring about transformation to unjust systems that oppress people.

2. Read Isaiah 9:1–7. In verse 6, Isaiah prophesied about the coming of Christ. How would the birth of Jesus change the world?

3. What is "the zeal of the LORD Almighty" (v. 7) going to accomplish?

4. Read Luke 2:1–20. The angel announced "good news of great joy that will be for all the people" (v. 10). Why was the coming of Christ good news for the poor?

5. In Luke 4:17–19, Jesus quoted Isaiah 61:1. What did Jesus claim to be his mission on earth?

6. In Luke 3:4–6, John the Baptist also quoted from the prophet Isaiah as he proclaimed the arrival of Jesus. What would result from Jesus' arrival on earth?

7. Read Mary's beautiful song of praise to God in Luke 1:46–55. What would happen to the hungry and rich as a result of the birth of Christ?

8. In what ways are you hungry today?

9. Like Mary, take a few minutes to lift praise to God for remembering those who are humble and hungry. As much as you can, try to identify yourself with the hungry.

Scripture Memory Verse

Isaiah 9:7: "Of the increase of his government and peace there will be no end. He will reign on David's throne and over his kingdom, establishing and upholding it with justice and righteousness from that time on and forever. The zeal of the LORD Almighty will accomplish this."

DAY 2
Righteousness and Justice

As we saw in our first week, righteousness and justice are often mentioned together in the Old Testament. In the New Testament, the Greek word *dikaiosune* carries within it the meaning of the word *justice*. Our translations usually render *dikaiosune* as simply *righteousness*. Since those of us in the Western world tend to take an individualistic view of life, many have thought of righteousness only in individual terms, as personal piety, being rightly related to God, when the word actually means much more.

1. Pray for God's light as you study the Scripture today. Ask him to help you gain a deeper understanding of what it means to do the work of justice.

2. Read Matthew 6:33. How does it change your understanding of the verse to substitute the word *justice* for *righteousness*?

3. Read James 3:18. How can Christians sow seeds of peace in the world?

4. Have you ever experienced having someone sow peace into your life? How?

5. Read Matthew 5:10. What persecutions do people face as they work for righteousness and justice today?

6. The word *blessed* in Matthew 5:10 can mean *happy*. Matthew makes the outlandish claim that people who are persecuted for the sake of righteousness and justice are actually happy and blessed. Have you found this to be true?

7. Matthew 6:10 is part of the prayer that Jesus used in teaching his disciples how to pray. What specifically could you pray for that would bring God's kingdom and will to your community?

8. Take a few minutes to pray for God's kingdom and will to be established in your community.

Scripture Memory Verse

Matthew 6:33: "But seek first his kingdom and his righteousness, and all these things will be given to you as well."

A City on a Hill

When I was a child, I used to love singing the chorus, "This Little Light of Mine." I held my finger proudly in the air, circling it above my head. I would let my little candle glow brightly until Jesus came. I wouldn't let Satan snuff it out. I was "gonna let it shine, let it shine, let it shine." I was personally going to make a difference in the world by letting my little light shine brightly. I sang with childlike determination.

It wasn't until later that I learned when Jesus said, "Let your light shine before men, that they may see your good deeds and praise your Father in heaven" (Matt. 5:16), he used the plural for the word *your*. Since *you* and *your* in the English language can be either singular or plural, we automatically tend to individualize it: I will shine my light alone. But Jesus was talking to a large crowd when he said those words, and he used the plural tense of *you*. In fact, he had told them they would be like "a city on a hill."

Today, we will reflect upon what can be accomplished as those who bear the light of Christ come together to shine the light of Christ like a city on a hill.

1. Pray for God's light as you study the Scripture today. Ask him to provide guidance about how you can share your light with others to be "a city on a hill."

2. Read Matthew 5:14–16. Why do you think Jesus used the concept of light to describe his followers?

3. Why would Christ followers be called the "light of the world"?

4. Have you ever witnessed an actual city set on a hill? What does it look like?

5. According to Matthew 5:16, what impact would followers of Christ make on the world if we combine the light of our lives as we reflect the light of Christ and place them high on lamp stands and hills instead of hiding them under bushels?

6. What groups of people are shining the light of good works in ways that the world is noticing and giving glory to God?

7. Take a few moments to pray. Ask God to show you what good deeds your church or group could do together in your community.

Scripture Memory Verse

Matthew 5:16: "Let your light shine before men, that they may see your good deeds and praise your Father in heaven."

Being the Light

Christine's four-year-old daughter is obsessed with flashlights. So Christine took her daughter to Wal-Mart to buy one. As Christine was paying for the flashlight her daughter begged, "Mommy, can we please go and find some darkness?"[1] Her daughter understood the purpose of light. We ought to understand the spiritual purpose of light. It's not to be scared of the darkness but to look for places of darkness and bring the light of Christ there.

Jesus calls us to be the light to the world by letting our lights shine like a city on a hill. The apostle Paul calls us to live in the light by letting the light of Christ permeate everything we say and do. We have the light that can illuminate the lives of those who are lost in the darkness. Today, we will reflect on light and darkness.

1. Pray for God's light as you study the Scripture today. Ask God to help you to understand what it means to live in the light and take it into dark places.

2. Read Ephesians 5:8–9. How were you living in darkness before you came to faith in Christ?

3. How has the light of Christ changed your life?

4. What is the fruit that becomes evident in the lives of people who are living as children of light?

5. Read Ephesians 2:8–10. What good works do you think God created you to do that would bring the light of Christ to dark places?

6. Read Galatians 5:6. The people were arguing about circumcision. What causes the most arguments in churches today?

7. What did the apostle Paul claim was the only thing that really mattered?

8. How have you experienced faith being expressed through love?

9. Take a few minutes to pray. Ask God how you can bring the light of Christ to dark places today.

Scripture Memory Verse

Galatians 5:6: "The only thing that counts is faith expressing itself through love."

Note

1. Christine Caine, Global Leadership Summit 2010 (lecture, Willow Creek Community Church, South Barrington, Ill., August 5, 2010), http://www.willowcreek.com/events/leadership/2010.

The Good News of the Gospel

Jesus proclaimed that the gospel would especially be good news for the poor. Not only would they have hope for eternal life in heaven, but the gospel would turn Christ followers into justice workers on earth. As believers take up the cross, they begin to follow in the way of Christ in service and love for those in need. Rather than hoarding and living lives of consumption, Christ followers become sacrificial in their love, giving to others as they recognize need.

Today, we will look at passages of Scripture that describe why the gospel is good news, especially for the poor.

1. Pray for God's light as you study the Scripture today. Ask him to show you how you can become even more involved in bringing good news to the poor.

2. Read Luke 4:18. Jesus claimed that he was sent to proclaim good news to the poor. Why would Jesus' coming be especially good news for people who were struggling economically?

3. Teresa of Avila is credited to have said, "Christ has no body but yours, no hands, no feet on earth but yours, yours are the eyes with which he looks compassion on this world." The church is Christ's body on earth today. What should the church be doing to carry out Jesus' mission?

4. Read Matthew 11:2–5. John instructed his disciples to ask Jesus if he was truly the Messiah. What did Jesus offer as proof that he was, indeed, the Son of God?

5. How would the world know by watching Jesus' followers that we are carrying out Jesus' mission to bring good news to the poor?

6. Take a few minutes to pray, asking God to show how you can move your church or group to be the evidence in the world that he loves all people, including the poor and broken.

Scripture Memory Verses

Matthew 11:4–5: "Jesus replied, 'Go back and report to John what you hear and see: The blind receive sight, the lame walk, those who have leprosy are cured, the deaf hear, the dead are raised, and the good news is preached to the poor.'"

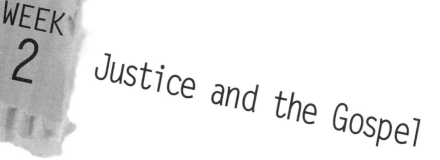

WEEK
2

Justice and the Gospel

GROUP DISCUSSION GUIDE

This week we studied many passages of Scripture that indicate that the gospel and justice are intricately related. The good news that Jesus brought to the world is not only good news for individual eternal salvation, but also that the systems of the world are being transformed as the church, the body of Christ on earth, continues the work of Jesus to care for the poor and oppressed and to seek their welfare.

1. As you start your group meeting today, pray for the Spirit to guide your discussion and reveal anything on which God desires you to focus.

2. Has individualism affected your understanding of righteousness? How?

3. How does Jesus' coming to earth and dying on the cross affect oppressive systems of injustice?

4. What relationship is there between the gospel and good works?

5. Christine Caine's daughter begged her mom to find some darkness so she could test out her new flashlight. Where is there darkness in your community?

6. According to Ephesians 5:8–9, what fruit will be displayed when Christians rise to be the light of Christ in the world?

7. How is the gospel good news for the poor?

8. What can your group do to bring good news to the poor in your community and throughout the world?

9. Pray together that God will provide direction to your group as you seek ways to be the light to people in your community who are experiencing social oppression.

This week we will study Nehemiah who organized the Hebrew community to repair the walls of Jerusalem. In *The Invisible*, I contrasted Nehemiah with Abraham's nephew, Lot, who failed to organize against the evil of his day (pp. 122–123).

Second Peter 2:7–8 says Lot was a righteous man who was "distressed by the filthy lives of lawless men (for that righteous man, living among them day after day, was tormented in his righteous soul by the lawless deeds he saw and heard)." I like another translation, which says, "He was vexed in his righteous soul day after day with their lawless deeds" (v. 8 RSV).

When God decided to destroy Sodom and Gomorrah because of their wickedness, Abraham was able to barter with God and garner a commitment that if ten righteous people could be found in the cities, God would not destroy the cities. Even though Lot was called a righteous man, he had not been able to influence others to join him to take a stand against the injustices of the cities.

Because Lot had been unable to mobilize even ten people in Sodom and Gomorrah to live godly lives, the cities were destroyed. The people of Sodom and Gomorrah have been remembered not only for their sexual deviance, but also because they "were arrogant, overfed and unconcerned; they did not help the poor and needy" (Ezek. 16:49).

You will not find any books on the leadership and impact of Lot, but dozens of books have been written about the life and leadership of Nehemiah. He saw the distress of the city of Jerusalem and started a movement to bring about change. He garnered resources from the government, conducted a reconnaissance mission to survey the problem, and mobilized a movement of people to rebuild the walls of Jerusalem. When he heard the outcry of the poor, he became "angry" (Neh. 5:6); "called together a large meeting" (v. 7); and told their oppressors, "What you are doing is not right. Shouldn't you walk in the fear of our God?" (v. 9). Nehemiah and his people have become known as "Repairer[s] of Broken Walls, Restorer[s] of Streets with Dwellings," just as Isaiah promised (Isa. 58:12). Nehemiah organized a movement to bring about transformation to the broken places of his city.

DAY 1

Nehemiah's Prayer

When Nehemiah learned about the condition of his city, he was distraught. He sat down and wept. But before he sprung into action, he fasted and prayed. I learned early in ministry the importance of seeking God before acting to right social wrongs, to be led by the Spirit rather than driven by need. In order for our actions to be led by the Spirit, we need to spend time praying and listening to God before we move into actions that will right social injustice.

Today we will study Nehemiah's prayer life.

1. Pray for God's light as you study the Scripture today. Ask God to help you understand the importance of praying before acting when seeking justice for the poor.

2. Read Nehemiah 1:3–5. What was the condition of Jerusalem and its people?

3. What is broken in your community?

4. How can you grow in your capacity to mourn over the brokenness?

5. How long did Nehemiah fast and pray?

6. Read Nehemiah 1:5, 8–10. What did Nehemiah affirm about God's character and commitment?

7. Read verses 6–7. Nehemiah confessed the sin of his people. In what ways might institutional sin have contributed to the brokenness of your community?

8. What does Nehemiah ask God for in verse 11?

9. Spend some time reflecting on the priority of prayer in your life. What can you learn from Nehemiah? Is God calling you to an extended time of fasting, confession, and prayer for your community?

Scripture Memory Verse

Nehemiah 1:11: "O Lord, let your ear be attentive to the prayer of this your servant and to the prayer of your servants who delight in revering your name."

Nehemiah Gathers Resources

Organizations and ministries that are trying to rebuild the city and care for those who are broken and cast aside by the world need to gather resources. Today, we will look at how Nehemiah was able to secure the funding he needed to pay for supplies and care for the workers who would rebuild the walls of the city.

1. Pray for God's light as you study the Scripture today. Ask him to give you insight into how kingdom work can and should be funded.

2. Read Nehemiah 2:1–10. What did Nehemiah do immediately after the king asked him what he wanted?

3. What did Nehemiah ask the king for?

4. Why did the king grant his request?

5. Read Nehemiah 5:17–19. What do you think Nehemiah's provisions for the workers would cost in today's economy?

6. According to Nehemiah 7:70–72, who, besides the king and governor, contributed to the work?

7. Leaders of kingdom building movements need to gather resources to care for the workers under their direction. Nehemiah used a mixture of government and private resources to fund the work. How might this apply to the funding of organizations and ministries today that are rebuilding communities?

8. Reflect on how you might invest your resources in a ministry or organization that is rebuilding your community.

Scripture Memory Verse

Luke 6:38: "Give, and it will be given to you. A good measure, pressed down, shaken together and running over, will be poured into your lap. For with the measure you use, it will be measured to you."

DAY 3

Nehemiah Recruits Workers

Nehemiah could not take on the massive task of rebuilding the walls of Jerusalem by himself. He needed to recruit workers and convince them to work together on the task. Nehemiah was a movement maker, a leader who inspired others to get involved. Let's see how he did it.

1. Pray for God's light as you study the Scripture today. Ask him to show you how you can recruit others to join you in a worthy cause.

2. Read Nehemiah 2:11–16. Nehemiah went out at night to examine the wall. Who did he take with him?

3. Why do you think he waited to recruit workers until after he had examined the wall?

4. Why do you think he examined the walls under the cover of night?

5. Read Nehemiah 2:17–18. How did Nehemiah convince others to join him in rebuilding the walls?

6. How did the people respond?

7. Many of us who grew up in the church might tend to take an individualistic approach to making a difference in the world. Why is it important that we join with others and work together when we are attempting to right the wrongs of systemic injustice?

8. Is there a movement for justice that God is calling you to start or join? How can you recruit others to get involved with you?

Scripture Memory Verse

Nehemiah 2:18: "I also told them about the gracious hand of my God upon me and what the king had said to me. They replied, 'Let us start rebuilding.' So they began this good work."

DAY 4

Nehemiah Stands Up to Opposition

Whenever we attempt to change the status quo in our communities, we can expect to face opposition. Nehemiah was immediately challenged by a group of men who wanted to stop him. They mocked him and ridiculed the workers. Nehemiah also had to deal with the discouragement of his own workers. Today, we will see how Nehemiah responded to encourage the workers and ward off the opposition.

1. Pray for God's light as you study the Scripture today. Ask him to show you how to respond to those who oppose your involvement in movements of Spirit-led social change.

2. Read Nehemiah 2:19–20. How did Sanballat, Tobiah, and Geshem try to discourage Nehemiah?

3. How did Nehemiah respond?

4. Read Nehemiah 4. How did Nehemiah's enemies increase the intensity of their opposition as they saw the work proceed?

5. How did Nehemiah respond?

6. Midway through a project, workers often become discouraged. What can a leader do to reenergize workers?

7. Nehemiah balanced prayer and prepared action. How can your group pray for and encourage the workers in the movements with which you are involved?

8. Spend some time praying for the groups in your community that are working to rebuild it.

Scripture Memory Verse

Romans 8:31: "If God is for us, who can be against us?"

Nehemiah Organizes the Builders

Nehemiah didn't just recruit the workers to rebuild the walls; he organized them and gave them each a role to play in the work. He took the huge task before him and broke it down into manageable parts. Each family was given a section of the wall to work on. Today, we will study how Nehemiah organized the people to successfully complete the task of rebuilding the walls.

1. Pray for God's light as you study the Scripture today. Ask God to show you how you can organize your family or group to take a place on the wall of building justice for the poor.

2. Read Nehemiah 3. About how many sections of the walls are mentioned with their assigned workers?

3. What types of people were involved in building the wall? What genders and occupations were represented?

4. How were the various work ethics of the participants described? Who were the slackers and who worked earnestly?

5. Nehemiah organized the people so that everyone had a job to do and all worked together in an organized way. Do you know leaders who have organized people to accomplish a great task? Describe what they accomplished and how they organized people to accomplish the task?

6. Justice is not a task we do individually. We must work together with others in an organized way. What movements are you involved in that are working to bring about social change?

Scripture Memory Verse

Isaiah 58:12: "Your people will rebuild the ancient ruins and will raise up the age-old foundations; you will be called Repairer of Broken Walls, Restorer of Streets with Dwellings."

Nehemiah: The Community Organizer

GROUP DISCUSSION GUIDE

This week we studied the work of Nehemiah, who gathered and organized the resources available to him—both finances and personnel—to begin to restore and rebuild his community. Nehemiah is an excellent example for those who want to bring God-centered change and justice to their neighborhoods and the world.

1. Open your group meeting in prayer, thanking God for the presence of the Holy Spirit and asking him to guide your discussion.

2. During the past week, we studied how Nehemiah organized a movement to rebuild the walls of Jerusalem. Ask the members of your group to share highlights from their personal studies. What are some of the characteristics of Nehemiah's response to the depressed condition of the city that stood out for you this week?

3. Nehemiah grieved and wept when he heard about the condition of the city of Jerusalem. What are some of the broken places in the world that cause you to grieve?

4. How do you allow yourself to grieve without becoming overwhelmed?

5. What did Nehemiah do with his grief?

6. What role did prayer play in Nehemiah's example of community organizing?

7. Nehemiah gathered resources from the king, governors, and people. How do you think kingdom work should be funded? What are some of the benefits or challenges of receiving government funding for rebuilding the city?

8. Nehemiah honored the workers by naming each one, detailing their accomplishments, and crediting them for their work. He made sure to record that the men of Tekoa repaired two sections of the wall (Neh. 3:5, 27) even though "their nobles would not put their shoulders to the work" (v. 5). How do you handle those who don't seem to be doing their part in the work for justice?

9. What can you do to honor those who are doing difficult work in tough places?

10. What are some things that might cause Christians who do justice work to become discouraged?

11. How can you encourage them?

12. How can your group serve together in a larger movement for justice?

13. Pray for the people you know who are leading movements of justice. Ask God how you can encourage them.

WEEK 4 Shalom: God's Justice Movement

Isaiah prophesied that Jesus would bring peace to the earth. He would be called the Prince of Peace, and there would be no end to the increase of his government and peace. Jesus would come and lead the world to peace. He would show us how to live. He would break down the walls that divide us and bring us together in a life of harmony and right relationships.

The Hebrew word for peace in the Old Testament is *shalom*. In Jewish culture, still today, people greet one another with the word *shalom*. Our English word *peace* doesn't do justice to the richness conveyed by the Hebrew term. It means much more: completeness, safety, welfare, soundness, contentment, tranquility, and harmony.

Cornelius Plantinga writes, "The webbing together of God, humans, and all creation in justice, fulfillment, and delight is what the Hebrew prophets call *shalom*. We translate it peace, but, it means far more than mere peace of mind or a cease-fire between enemies. In the Bible, shalom means *universal flourishing, wholeness, delight*—a rich state of affairs in which natural needs are satisfied and natural gifts fruitfully employed. . . . Shalom, in other words is the way things ought to be."[1]

Timothy Keller teaches that when God created the world, he laid it out like a garment (Ps. 102:25–26). A piece of fabric is made up of hundreds or thousands of threads woven together. The world God created is billions of entities intricately woven together by God, with interdependence and harmony. Keller says the work of the peacemaker is to participate in God's work to reweave and repair the fabric of creation in those places where the fabric of society has unraveled.[2]

This week, we will study passages of Scripture that describe God's overarching mission to bring shalom to earth through the church and to see what the world would look like if God was in charge.

Notes

1. Cornelius Plantinga, Jr., *Not the Way It's Supposed to Be: A Breviary of Sin* (Grand Rapids, Mich.: Eerdmans, 1995), 10.
2. Timothy Keller, "Doing Justice" (Resurgence), 54 min., 22 sec.; MPEG, http://www.theresurgence.com/r_r_2006_session_eight_audio_keller.

Fishing with Nets

Jesus was calling his disciples to follow him in Matthew 4 when he said, "Follow me and I will make you fishers of men." We personalized the "Fishers of Men" song as children by pretending we had a rod and reel in our hands.

Jesus' disciples didn't fish with fishing rods but with nets. Fishing with nets is not something you do by yourself. The disciples would have imagined joining others to stand at their place in a big net that God was spreading across the world. Drawing in the least and lost to Christ is done together with others. It is in community that we draw people to Christ. Jesus was teaching a network model of caring for people.

1. Pray for God to guide you as you study the Scripture today. Ask him to show you how you can take your place in the network of care and love that he is casting over the world.

2. Read Luke 4:18–19. In these verses, Jesus quoted from Isaiah 61:1 and 42:7 to announce the work he was about to establish on earth. He also alluded to the Year of Jubilee described in Leviticus 25 that we studied earlier. According to these verses, what was Jesus' mission on earth?

3. What should Christians be doing as we continue the work of Christ on earth?

4. Read Psalm 27:10. What will God do for people who are forsaken by their parents?

5. In this verse, the phrase "receive me" is rendered "to gather into association with others." How is God using you, your church, and your friends to "gather into association with others" those who have been neglected or cast aside by their families?

6. How does this image of taking your place at a net differ from the way you have thought about bringing the lost into the supportive family of God?

7. Take a few minutes to pray. Ask God who you can join to provide a network of loving support for those who are lost and struggling.

Scripture Memory Verse

Psalm 27:10: "Though my father and mother forsake me, the LORD will receive me."

Blessed Are the Poor

It seems like an oxymoron, doesn't it? Why would Jesus say the poor are blessed? If the poor are blessed, why do we try so hard to avoid poverty? Did Jesus really say the poor are blessed, or just the poor in spirit? Matthew and Luke probably heard the same words from Jesus' mouth. Luke quoted Jesus as saying, "Blessed are the poor," while Matthew added the words, "in spirit." Regardless, Jesus was implying that we all have something to learn from the experience of poverty, whether physically or spiritually.

Many have found among the poor, people whose faith was so forged in the furnaces of adversity that they can still trust God when many of us would melt with fear. Money can provide a semblance of insulation from some problems, but sooner or later, we all—even the rich—come to the end of our untried faith and need more experienced warriors to hold us up and show us how to reach out to God. That's when someone who's been through it becomes your best friend. Jesus' first beatitude, "Blessed are the poor in spirit," describes those who know they are nothing without God. But they are so rich in faith that "theirs is the kingdom of heaven" (Matt. 5:3). In most cases, these "poor" people generously share what they do have even with the "rich." Experience friends like that and you will understand what Jesus meant when he proclaimed, "Blessed are the poor."

1. Pray for God's light as you study the Scripture today. Ask him to show you how you can experience the blessing of recognizing your own poverty.

2. When you think back over your life, have there been times when it seemed you were going through difficulties but you experienced God's presence in a special way?

3. Read Matthew 5:1–12 and Luke 6:20–22. Who did Jesus claim to be blessed?

4. Why were they blessed?

5. In Luke 6:23, what did Jesus urge people who were blessed in their difficulties to do and why?

6. Read Luke 6:24–26. What warning did Jesus give to those who didn't recognize and experience their own poverty?

7. Make a list of the commandments of Jesus in Luke 6:27–38.

8. What will be the results of following those commands?

9. Take a few minutes to pray. Ask God to show you ways you can act on these commands today.

Scripture Memory Verse

Matthew 5:3: "Blessed are the poor in spirit, for theirs is the kingdom of heaven."

The Promise of Future Justice

In *The Invisible*, I wrote about an era in Christianity when Bible believing Christians, especially white, middle, and upper class Christians, strayed away from the biblical mandate to work for justice for the poor (ch. 2). Those of us who learned the "personal piety" Christianity of the '50s, '60s, and '70s knew how to recite John 3:16 from memory. We didn't, however, memorize 1 John 3:16–17: "This is how we know what love is: Jesus Christ laid down his life for us. And we ought to lay down our lives for our brothers. If anyone has material possessions and sees his brother in need but has no pity on him, how can the love of God be in him?"

The central error of the mainstream Christian church during this era is that it held a truncated view of the gospel. Jesus' proclamation that he had been anointed by the Spirit to preach good news to the poor, proclaim freedom to the prisoners, give sight to the blind, and release the oppressed is as much the message of the gospel as the eternal salvation of one's soul. Eternal life for believers in Christ starts the moment we align ourselves with Christ's redemptive work on the cross and take up our cross to follow him in laying down our lives for others.

Today, we will study a passage of Scripture that describes what the world will be like when Jesus is fully in charge. It is a vision of the world the way God intends it to be.

1. Take a few minutes to pray, asking God to show you how you can participate in his plan for a redeemed world.

2. Read Isaiah 65:17–25. According to verses 18–19, what will characterize the new earth?

3. What does verse 20 indicate about the health of infants and the elderly?

4. What do verses 21–22 have to say about the availability of homes and food?

5. What do verses 22–23 predict about meaningful work?

6. Where in the world today are children being born to misfortune?

7. What does verse 23 have to say about family life?

8. What does verse 24 indicate about God's involvement in the lives of people in this redeemed world?

9. According to verse 25, even the animals will be at peace. Since we know from Genesis 3 that the serpent is often used to represent Satan, we might assume that the lion and lamb could represent the strong and weak. What might this verse be revealing about crime and violence in the world as God meant it to be?

10. Spend some time envisioning the kind of world described in Isaiah 65. Ask God to show you places in your community that are especially far removed from the world as God intends it to be and how you might be involved in working to bring about change to those environments.

Scripture Memory Verse

Isaiah 65:18: "But be glad and rejoice forever in what I will create, for I will create Jerusalem to be a delight and its people a joy."

DAY 4

Pray for Shalom

Walter Brueggemann once said, "Shalom . . . can function as a theology of hope, a large-scale promissory vision of what will one day surely be. As a vision of an assured future, the substance of shalom is crucial, for it can be a resource against both despair and an overly eager settlement for an unfinished system."[1]

In our passage today, the prophet Jeremiah tells the Jews held captive in Babylon to seek the peace and prosperity of the city to which they had been carried into exile. "Pray to the LORD for it, because if it prospers, you too will prosper" (Jer. 29:7). Today, we will study the context of that verse and reflect upon what it means to seek peace and prosperity for those who struggle in impoverished communities throughout the world. We will be challenged to pray for shalom.

1. Pray that God will open your heart and mind to the meaning of shalom and equip you to be a peacemaker.

2. Read Jeremiah 29:4–7. Jeremiah was writing to the Jews who had been forcefully deported from Judah and carried away to Babylon by Nebuchadnezzar. They were held captive in Babylon under difficult circumstances for seventy years. Jeremiah encouraged them to make the best of a bad situation. What were they told to do in verse 6?

3. According to verses 4 and 7, who was ultimately responsible for the exile of the Jews to Babylon?

4. In verse 7, God told the people who were going through the pain of slavery in Babylon to pray for the peace of the city where they were taken captive. The oppressed were to pray for the peace of the oppressor. In Luke 6:28, Jesus said we are to "bless those who curse [us], pray for those who mistreat [us]." Who might God ask you to pray for so that your enemies may be at peace?

5. According to Jeremiah 29:7, what will happen to you if your enemy prospers?

6. Can you think of places and systems in our world where the fabric of God's shalom has been frayed?

7. What can you do to help build the shalom of God in those places?

8. Take a few moments to pray for the peace of those who are making life difficult for you and others throughout the world that are in distressing circumstances. Ask God to show you what you can do to build shalom in the places of the world where systems are broken.

Scripture Memory Verse

Jeremiah 29:7: "Also, seek the peace and prosperity of the city to which I have carried you into exile. Pray to the LORD for it, because if it prospers, you too will prosper."

Note

1. Walter Brueggemann, *Peace*, Understanding Biblical Themes (St. Louis, Mo.: Chalice Press, 2001), 5.

Wisdom to Administer Justice

My friend Cindy made a discovery that surprised me. She read through the Bible and highlighted every passage that referred to justice and care for the poor. "Do you know what Solomon asked God for?" she asked me.

"Sure," I replied, confident in my Sunday school education. "He asked God for wisdom and God gave him the bonus of riches and honor."

I was surprised to learn from Cindy that Solomon had asked God for more than just wisdom. Today, we will look more deeply into Solomon's request.

1. Pray that God will give you a heart of justice for the poor today.

2. Read 1 Kings 3:9–15. According to verse 15, Solomon had a dream about a conversation between him and God. According to verses 9 and 11, what did Solomon ask God to give him in the dream?

3. How did Solomon's request make God feel?

4. After the situation with the two women and baby, what did the people observe about Solomon (v. 3:28)?

5. What situations are you aware of or experiencing right now in which you need "wisdom from God to administer justice" (v. 28)?

6. Frederick Buechner said, "The place God calls you to is the place where your deep gladness and the world's deep hunger meet."[1] What might God be calling you to do?

7. Like Solomon, ask God to give you wisdom to administer justice. Take some time to pray and listen to God's whisper in your heart about what you have been called to do to bring justice to a hurting world.

Scripture Memory Verses

Proverbs 31:8–9: "Speak up for those who cannot speak for themselves, for the rights of all who are destitute. Speak up and judge fairly; defend the rights of the poor and needy."

Note

1. Frederick Buechner, *Wishful Thinking: A Seekers ABC* (San Francisco, Calif.: HarperOne, 1993), 119.

Shalom: God's Justice Movement

GROUP DISCUSSION GUIDE

Open your group meeting in prayer, thanking God for the presence of the Holy Spirit and asking him to guide your discussion.

This week, we studied passages of Scripture that give evidence to the work of God in the world to bring justice and peace. We have only to watch the news or drive through certain communities to realize that there is a tremendous gap in the good news of God's kingdom and the challenging issues that are so obvious in our inner cities and impoverished communities throughout the world.

1. As you gather with your group, ask God to guide your conversation and give you practical insight as to how you can participate in his overarching mission to bring justice to the poor.

2. Ask the members of your group to share highlights from their personal studies.

3. How has individualistic thinking about evangelism and discipleship shaped the way you have approached reaching the lost?

4. What are some practical ways you can learn to fish with nets?

5. Where in the world is the fabric of society most frayed and broken?

6. What groups of people are experiencing social oppression?

7. The two sins that are mentioned most often in Scripture are idolatry (putting other things and people before God) and lack of care for the poor. How are these sins related to one another?

8. We read about God's vision for a redeemed world in Isaiah 65:17–25. What would have to change in the world for this vision to become realized?

9. What is God leading your group to do as a result of this study?

Conclusion

Congratulations! You have successfully concluded this in-depth study from God's Word regarding justice for the poor. I pray you have been moved in some way by this study to take action on behalf of the less fortunate. Justice involves working for change in the systems of the world that bring oppression and poverty to so many. It is a challenge we cannot face alone. That's why God instituted the church, Christ's body on earth, for us to work together. To take up our place on a net and to become part of movements and networks that are working together for change. The church is the largest grassroots movement of compassionate people in the world. We have been commissioned to work with God to right the wrongs of systemic evil. We have what it takes to bring transformation to entire communities through the power of the Holy Spirit. I believe we have been called by God to do so.

God desires justice. He has prepared good works for us to do. When we shine our lights together, we become a city on a hill. We join with others to spread a network of compassion and justice throughout the world, and the world takes notice and glorifies God. Welcome to the justice journey. You will never be the same.